BURN ALIVE

MICHELLE JESTER

ISBN: 978-1-964026-15-2 (paperback)
ISBN: 978-1-964026-16-9 (ebook)

BURN ALIVE

MH

MICHTER HOUSE
PUBLISHING
an imprint of
Rope Swing Publishing

www.ropeswingpublishing.com

Because You say so...

Luke 5:4-7

Letter from the Author

I usually put my author's note at the back of a book, but this one is different.

When I woke up in a sweat and jotted down what I could remember of a dream, I knew I would start this book. I dream a lot. Many of my novels and some of my nonfiction stem from dreams. Are they all inspired by God? I think all good things are inspired by God, so, I give Him the glory! However, some dreams I know deep in my spirit are one hundred percent, without a doubt, given with fire by God. This book is born of one of those dreams.

My prayer from the beginning has been that it would be fuel. I wrote this because I know God placed it in me to do so. My hope is that it fuels your faith, your passion, and the dreams God planted deep inside of you. I didn't write it because I have mastered revival, I wrote it because I'm desperate for it. I've lived through the flicker and felt the fire dim. I've tasted the ashes of disappointment and dryness. But I've also seen what happens when God breathes into my life again.

About a year and a half ago, I was running nonstop. Social media took a lot of time and effort. It had become so important to my brand and business that it had slowly become more of my output than the output of my *purpose*. I prayed and felt that instead of social media being my by-product; it had become the product. It was difficult because I worried that in easing off of social media at all, my sales, brand, or reach would take a major hit. But I knew deep down that I'd already taken a much deeper hit by allowing it to become a top priority over my purpose, and not just a helper of it.

So, I surrendered it to God. Did I still post? Yes. However, I posted seldom and did so in joy and excitement, rather than out of a calendar telling me to. There were also times I wanted to post something because I felt the need out of habit. I am not going to lie and say that it wasn't uncomfortable to slow the posting, because it was. I *wanted* to share, but I knew *the sharing* had taken priority over *the doing.* Something had to change. I knew it was a time of renewal for me. A freshening of God in my direction and purpose. It was also a time of rest.

In that space, I began to refocus on God and His presence, and time with others that didn't always require a happy selfie on social media. I spent more time connecting with God and His people. Not just Christians... because we are all God's children. I finished so many projects that had been inching along, I completed many open-ended projects. All of which had been at a stalemate.

Do I believe taking a social media break is for everyone? I'm definitely not saying that. But I do believe there is something in all of our lives that distracts us from *the* life. From the heart of the purpose

God put in us. I can't say what that is for everyone else, but I do know it requires a surrendered heart. No matter the fear of what letting go means. I've let go of a lot of things in the past year and a half, things I didn't want to. Things I was holding onto. Relationships that weren't working, business avenues that weren't producing, and a schedule that was so tight, I had to "fit in" things that should've taken precedence.

I am actively trying to surrender them all to God.

It wasn't comfortable giving all of those things to God, but I knew it would be a freedom I had never known. I've seen what His presence can do in full surrender.

That's what I believe for all of us. I believe we are all in a new state of personal revival.

I believe our best days in His presence are not behind us, but ahead of us. I believe that the hunger stirring inside of you is not an accident, it's a fire. I believe the voice in you that has become a whisper, is moving into a battle cry. You were not created to drift through life half-lit, half-alive, and fully exhausted. You were born to burn, shine, and to carry His glory into every space you enter.

I want you to know God sees you. He knows the fire in us, the purpose He has for us, and He knows how to make it burn brighter than ever before. No moment of pain, no season of delay or loss, and no sin too deep can disqualify you from His revival power. His mercy is fierce. His grace is deeper than the deepest place you've ever fallen. His love is relentless. He still chooses you. He still calls your name. And more importantly, He will equip you.

You don't need a title to carry the fire. You don't need a platform to make an impact. You need a heart that says, "Jesus, whatever You want, I'm all in." That is where revival begins. That is where joy is restored, and that is where the flame never goes out.

So, run. Run with passion. Do everything with passion: be holy, worship with all you've got, love with your whole heart, and pray without holding back. Speak truth with compassion and courage. Wherever you go, let people feel the warmth of God upon your life. Let them see the difference, taste the joy, and be drawn to the fire in you. Let that fire point them straight to Him.

I love you deeply, even if we've never met, because we are family in this great Kingdom of God. We were born for such a time as this.

We were born to burn alive,

Michelle

INTRODUCTION

Wake the Flame

Something in you knows there is more. You feel it in the moments of stillness, when the noise fades and the ache rises to the surface. Maybe your voice has dimmed in the last few years. You remember what it used to feel like when your heart *burned* for God. You remember the days when Scripture felt alive and prayer wasn't a chore but a lifeline. When worshiping God, no matter where you were, was natural, not guarded. Worship wasn't just a "fix it" but a "lead it." You remember when praise wasn't just words, they caused you to tremble in awe and weep in joy. That fire was real. It was holy. It was the evidence of the Holy Living Spirit of God dwelling inside of you. Somewhere along the way, though, the flame dimmed. Maybe it's not gone but fading. Maybe it went out entirely, like a windstorm swept through your soul and left only ashes behind. Whatever the cause, however the severity, you are here, reading these words, knowing deep down that you desire it again.

Throughout Scripture, fire has always marked God's presence. From the burning bush that spoke to Moses, to the pillar of fire that led the Israelites through the wilderness, to the tongues of fire that fell on the early Church at Pentecost, fire has never been just a symbol. It is the language of heaven. It is the evidence of divine encounter. Where there is fire, there is God. Where there is no fire, something is missing.

Many of us have learned how to manage a life on a low flame, especially in the age of political correctness. We love God, attend church, sing the songs, post the verses, and smile through it all while quietly, or even unintendedly, allowing spiritual fatigue to fester in our bones. We wonder where the joy went. Wonder why we aren't as productive or excited. We question why intimacy with God feels distant and we find that we've settled for temporary distractions instead of confronting the deeper truth. God has not moved. He has not grown quiet. He is still a consuming fire. The problem is not in Him. The problem is often in our own surrender.

Revival always begins with the honest confession that we have grown cold. There is no shame in this realization. It happens to us all. But there is an open invitation waiting. The invitation to return. The invitation to repent. The invitation to be reignited. In Acts 3:19-20, the Word says, "Repent, then, and turn to God, so that your sins may be wiped out, that times of refreshing may come from the Lord." This is not just about behavior. It is about posture. Repentance is not punishment. It is the sacred key that unlocks refreshment. True revival does not begin in a crowded stadium. It begins in a heart that says, "God, I want

You more than anything else."

We were not made for lukewarm living. Jesus Himself warned the church in Laodicea in Revelation 3:15-16, "I know your deeds, that you are neither cold nor hot. I wish you were either one or the other! So, because you are lukewarm, neither hot nor cold, I am about to spit you out of my mouth." This is not harsh. It is holy. God is not interested in halfhearted faith. He is not calling us to religious performance. He is calling us to be ablaze with love, fueled by the Spirit, given to compassion, and surrendered in obedience. He is calling us to burn alive.

Revivals started in places where people were searching for God. The Reformation was born out of strong beliefs, not ease. Through impassioned preaching, public displays of repentance, and a drive for spiritual purity, the Great Awakenings unfolded. The Jesus Movement wasn't born from eloquent speeches, but from raw vulnerability and life-changing experiences of grace. What marked these movements was not fancy lights or flawless music. It was hunger. It was repentance. Not manufactured fire, but the unmistakable presence of

God showing up in power, burning away apathy and igniting passion.

We are facing it again. Not just collectively, but personally. Homes filled with prayer, no matter the circumstances. Marriages fueled by God's presence, no matter the issues. Young people ablaze with unshakable conviction, no matter the current culture. Leaders who lead from the secret place, not the spotlight. Believers who do not just quote Scripture but live it. Individuals praying for another without fear of offense. We need the kind of fire that spreads.

The good news is that revival is not a historical relic. It is not a once-in-a-generation phenomenon. It is the desire of God's heart. He wants to revive us more than we want to be revived. The question is not whether He *will* move. The question is whether we *will* make room. Revival cannot live where pride does. It cannot thrive in the presence of compromise. It is not sustained by talent or structure. It is sustained by humility, holiness, and hunger.

Romans 13:11-12 says, "The hour has already come for you to wake up from your slumber, because our salvation is nearer now than when we first believed. The night is nearly over; the day is almost here." This is not a casual reminder. *It is a holy alarm.* Wake up. Shake off spiritual slumber. Step into the light. The fire you once had is not lost forever. The joy that once poured from your soul can return. The intimacy you thought faded beyond repair can be rekindled. God restores, revives, and breathes life where there was death. He raises dry bones and sets hearts on fire.

This book will not hand you a formula. It will not offer a checklist. Won't shove religious teachings down your throat. It can only point you to the One who still ignites the willing.

Let this be your turning point. Let this be the season where the fire returns, not for a moment, but for a lifetime. We need it, and the world needs it. Revival is not a feeling. It is a surrender. It is not reserved for church services. It is for your ordinary, everyday life. It is for your soul, your voice, your hands, your future, and your purpose.

So, open your heart. Lay everything down. Let the ashes get swept away by the wind of renewal. Let the Word cut, and the presence heal. Let the fire of Heaven fall again.

Let it fall on you and burn you alive.

CHAPTER 1

When the Flame Flickers

You may not even know when it happened. The change came subtly. You wanted to pray for someone, but worried that it would be taken as judgment. You wanted to post a scripture, but in the culture, worried that it would make you look like a hater. What was once blazing and bright had turned to embers in a world where Christ was needed more than ever and rejected just as fiercely.

Maybe the passion that once stirred

you to tears now barely moves you. You worship, but it often feels mechanical. Your prayers sound hollow. You know all the right words, but your soul feels distant from the One who used to set it ablaze.

This is the ache of a flickering flame. It is not that you stopped believing. You still believe. It is not that you walked away entirely. You are still showing up, still trying, still hoping. Yet deep within, there is a nagging sense that you have grown quiet in your faith. You remember how it used to feel when you encountered God with fresh wonder and the world with vigor. You remember when repentance felt like freedom, not shame. You remember joy.

The world has made repentance an evil word, so many quit talking about it. Yet, it is the only step forward. The most important step before God almighty that surrenders and transforms your life.

In Revelation 2, Jesus speaks to the church in Ephesus. He honors their hard work, their discernment, their endurance. He acknowledges that they have held onto truth. Then He says the words that pierce deeper than any compliment ever could: "Yet I hold this against you: You have forsaken the love you had at first." It is possible to be right and still be wrong. It is possible to do the work of faith and yet drift from the passion of it. Jesus did not accuse them of failure in doctrine or discipline. He called them back to desire.

It's not always about being rebellious. Sometimes it is about routine. It is easy to replace wonder with busyness. It is easy to trade awe for activity. Slowly, almost imperceptibly, the fire dims as we go through the motions and forget the reason behind it all. It's easy to fall into the trap of fitting into the world, thinking your voice will be heard through the empathy you have for others, versus being a light of truth to the world, showing the repentance and glory of God.

I love God. I have a passionate love for God. I am thrilled to be living my purpose. Still, I had to be refreshed. Something wasn't quite right. People often say I'm a firecracker, always doing so much. And I do. It's part of my personality. I love staying busy, I often feel inspired, and crave staying on the move. I know God has equipped me for it. But I get fatigued, like everyone else. I have to step away from it sometimes and realize that God doesn't care how much I'm doing over how much I am letting Him do in me.

God never called us to manage our faith, or the faith of others. He called us to live it with fire. The flicker is not a sign of failure. It is a signal that something higher is missing. Maybe not entirely missing, but also not fully present. It is the whisper of the Holy Spirit calling us back, not to obligation, but to intimacy. The first step in revival is not trying harder. It is admitting the truth. The flame is flickering, and we want it back.

"Create in me a pure heart, O God, and renew a steadfast spirit within me... Restore to me the joy of Your salvation and grant me a willing spirit, to sustain me." Psalm 51:10-12 was not written by a man who had lost belief. They were written by a man who had lost his fire. David, once full of worship and wonder, found himself dry, broken, and guilty. He did not run from God. He ran to Him. He did not offer excuses. He offered a plea.

This is where revival begins, in honesty with God. Not in performance. Not in appearances. Not in our work or output. In a humble, heart-wrenching confession:

I miss the fire and I want it back. When you pray for that, God listens. Not with condemnation, but with compassion. He knows exactly how to breathe on flickering flames so that they ignite with glory.

In Isaiah 42:3, it says, "A bruised reed He will not break, and a smoldering wick He will not snuff out." God is not here to shame your flicker. He is here to fan it into flame. What feels like failure is actually opportunity. When the fire is low, the hunger grows. When the light dims, the longing deepens. The ache you feel is not something to hide. It is something to follow. That ache is holy.

None of us were ever meant to live in spiritual survival mode. Going through the motions is not our calling. We are not here to manage our faith like a fragile possession. We are here to be consumed. Hebrews 12:29 declares that "our God is a consuming fire." He is not distant. He is not dull. He burns with glory. His love is fierce. His presence is weighty. His holiness is purifying. He invites you into the furnace of transformation.

The world is full of noise, distractions, and cheap substitutes. It is full of people who believe in the principles of Christianity but have not surrendered to them. The world offers quick fixes and empty thrills. It numbs what it cannot heal. It entertains while it exhausts. No wonder the fire in so many hearts grows dim. We watch as people judge others, instead of letting the Holy Spirit convict them of their own wrongdoings. Hypocrisy runs rampant, pointing fingers at other Christians for "selling out" to the world, but using social media platforms that often sell out Christianity itself to do so. Don't mistake what I am saying. I believe social media gives us a platform and voice to bring the truth to others. That must happen. I am only saying that, in judging others for the same things we do ourselves in different ways, many of us fail to see through the log in our own eyes. I'm also not saying to ignore sin. But when we say we hate the sin and love the sinner, but constantly throw eggs in their face, we are doing the opposite.

It's important to know that repentance and judgment are not the same.

Repentance is an invitation from God, a loving call to turn from what harms us and return to what heals us. It is rooted in mercy and hope, showing people that change is possible because God's grace is bigger than their sin. When we speak to others about repentance, we can do it with tenderness and humility, remembering that we also stand in need of grace. We point to the One who forgives, not to ourselves as the standard. John 5:45

Judgment, on the other hand, focuses on condemning rather than restoring. It places us in the seat of a critic rather than the arms of a shepherd. When we judge someone for their sin, we often speak from superiority and fear, which can drive them farther from God rather than closer. When we judge ourselves, we force a wedge between the sacrifice of Jesus in our life. Judgment does not offer a way forward. It only points out failure.

Speaking about repentance with compassion is very different. It reflects the heart of Christ, who told the truth about sin yet welcomed sinners with open arms. It looks someone in the eye and says, "You are loved, you are called higher, and there is freedom for you." It is honest, but it is also kind. When our words are full of mercy, people can sense that God is drawing them, not shaming them.

Our humility and understanding of repentance in our own lives and our words become a reflection of His patience and His truth to others. We do not excuse sin, but we also do not crush people under the weight of it. We invite, we encourage, and we walk with them toward a better way, trusting that the Holy Spirit is the one who convicts and transforms. In this way, repentance becomes a gift offered in love, never a weapon used in judgment.

I am far from perfect. However, sometimes I strive for it, instead of surrendering it. We cannot live lit if we are constantly striving to be perfect or pulled into condemning others, instead of receiving conviction ourselves and spreading God's amazing Grace. That drains our oil and douses our flame. That culture does not fuel revival. It fights it. If you want the fire back, you have to turn from the things that have quietly smothered it in you.

This is not about shame. It is about choice. You can choose again. You can ask for more. God never says no to the heart that genuinely longs for Him. In

Jeremiah 29:13, He promises, "You will seek Me and find Me when you seek Me with all your heart." Not halfway. Not casually. All your heart. That is where fire lives.

You seek. Not "you seek to convert others." When you are full of God's fire, others will see it and be transformed by it.

God can reignite what has gone stale. He can restore what you thought was lost. He can awaken what you believed was dead. Let your heart say what your mouth may be afraid to: I want the fire again. I want to feel Your nearness. I want to tremble in Your presence. I want to weep over Your goodness. I want to live fully alive. I want to surrender again.

You are not too late or too far. The flickering flame is not your failure. It is your call. Let the whisper become a roar.

CHAPTER 2

Wake Up, Sleeper

There is a moment in every believer's life when heaven issues a holy alarm. I believe that time is now for us all.

The Apostle Paul speaks directly to this in Romans 13:11–12: "The hour has already come for you to wake up from your slumber, because our salvation is nearer now than when we first believed. The night is nearly over; the day is almost here." These are not poetic lines. They are a spiritual jolt. Paul is writing to believers who have become sluggish, distracted, and complacent. He is not scolding them. He is sounding the alarm.

There is a difference between rest and slumber. Rest is intentional, restorative, and holy. I spent the last year and a half "resting." Slumber is unintentional, passive, and dangerous. I've spent time there as well. Many believers fell asleep with their eyes open. Still attending services. Still say grace at meals. Still wear the name of Jesus. Yet deep inside, spirits have grown duller and convictions have softened. The fire has nearly gone silent.

Spiritual sleep is subtle. It does not happen in a single moment. It creeps in over time. We compromise in small ways. We trade sacred rhythms for convenient habits. We begin to tolerate in the world what once grieved us. We silence the whisper of the Spirit to avoid discomfort for others and ourselves. Eventually, we find ourselves going through the motions, unaware that the passion we once had is now buried under the weight of spiritual fatigue.

God never intended His people to live half-awake. He created us to walk in the light, to be alert, to be watchful. In Matthew 25, Jesus tells the parable of ten virgins waiting for the bridegroom. All ten were invited. All ten had lamps. Yet only five were wise enough to keep their lamps burning. The other five grew careless. They fell asleep without oil, unprepared for the moment the bridegroom arrived. When He came, it was too late. The door was shut.

This is a sobering parable. It reminds us that invitation is not enough. Passion must be sustained. Flame must be guarded. Intimacy with God is not something we casually drift into. It must be *pursued, protected, and prioritized*. Wakefulness is not about striving. It is about awareness. We must stay aware of God's presence and resist cultural pressures that might tempt us to compromise.

The world can be loud and relentless. It constantly demands our attention and pulls us away. It urges us to comply, to assimilate, and to compromise our principles for tolerance or convenience. It also calls us to be loud in pointing fingers at others, to throw eggs, and it calls us to say hateful things in the name of religion. If we are not careful, we will slowly fall asleep to the things of God in our very souls while being wide awake to the world. We will become more familiar with trends than with truth. More focused on others than ourselves. More passionate about causes than about Christ. More stirred by emotion than by the eternal.

Ephesians 5:14 says, "Wake up, sleeper, rise from the dead, and Christ will shine on you." This is the voice of God echoing through generations. Wake up. Rise. Let light shine on you. The call to wake up is not about shame. It is about grace. God does not shake us to condemn us. He shakes us to restore us. He interrupts our slumber. He knows the fire we once carried. He knows the joy that has faded. He knows the intimacy we once fought for.

There is mercy in the personal shaking of our intimacy with God. There is hope in the interruption. *Every holy awakening begins with a disruption.* God breaks into our comfort to bring us into His glory. He tears down what numbs us so that He can build up what transforms us.

The early church understood this. In Acts 2, the disciples were gathered in one place when suddenly the sound of a rushing wind filled the room. Fire rested on their heads, and they were filled with the Holy Spirit. They were not asleep. They were expectant. They were waiting. When God moved, they did not hesitate. They stepped into the streets and boldly proclaimed the truth.

God still moves that way. He still fills the expectant and pours fire on those who prepare room for Him. Revival comes to those who are awake. It comes to the hungry, the watchful, the ones who refuse to let sleep steal their calling.

This is not the time to drift. This is not the time to silence the personal conviction we feel. *This is the time to stir your soul and reclaim your urgency.* Romans 13 speaks with such clarity: "The night is nearly over; the day is almost here." The clock is ticking. Eternity is advancing. We must not waste our days in spiritual drowsiness. We must rise.

To wake up spiritually is to repent of distraction. It is to clear the clutter of the soul. It is to turn off the noise that keeps us numb and tune into the voice that calls us higher. It is to say, "God, I want to live with eyes wide open to Your presence."

Jesus is not returning for a sleepy

bride. He is returning for one who is radiant and ready. He is returning for those whose hearts are burning with love, whose hands are filled with oil, whose eyes are fixed on Him.

If you feel the flicker in your spirit, do not ignore it. That is the Spirit of God waking you up. That is mercy. That is grace. That is the first spark of revival.

Let this be your moment. Lay aside everything that distracts you. Turn from what dampens your desire. Silence the lies that told you to be silent.

Let the light of Christ shine on you. Let the alarm ring in your soul.

The fire is calling.

CHAPTER 3

The Breath of Heaven

Every believer faces a time when their soul begins to thirst in a way that nothing on earth can satisfy. It is not physical exhaustion, though the body may feel tired. It is deeper. It is the longing of a spirit that has run dry from too many days of going through the motions. This kind of thirst does not go away with sleep or a vacation. It can only be quenched by something eternal. It can only be satisfied by the breath of Heaven.

Acts 3:19–20 offers a divine remedy. "Repent, then, and turn to God, so that your sins may be wiped out, that times of refreshing may come from the Lord." This is more than a comforting passage. It is a prescription for the weary. The phrase "times of refreshing" in the Greek is "anapsyxis," which means a cooling, a reviving, a recovery of breath. This is the living breath of God being poured out on a soul that is suffocating in sin, shame, or spiritual dryness.

We often think of repentance as something heavy. Many associate it with guilt and regret. Yet here, repentance is the gateway to breath. It is the holy door through which God enters and revives. Repentance clears the lungs of what pollutes. It empties the heart of what hinders. It makes space for God to breathe again in you and revive.

Think about the first breath Adam ever took. He did not come alive because of effort. He came alive because God breathed into him. Genesis 2:7 says, "Then the Lord God formed the man of dust from the ground and breathed into his nostrils the breath of life, and the man became a living creature." The dust did not decide to move. It came alive when Heaven inhaled and exhaled into it. That same breath still brings life today. When your spirit feels like dust, you do not need self-help. You need the Spirit of God.

We are not designed to live on yesterday's breath. We cannot thrive on yesterday's encounter. Just as our bodies need constant oxygen, our souls need constant breath from Heaven. Many are gasping spiritually and do not even know it. The pace of life, the weight of performance, the distractions of culture, and the residue of sin can leave us breathless. Over time, we grow used to living on empty. We forget what it felt like to be full.

The early Church did not run on talent. It ran on breath. In Acts 2, the Holy Spirit came like a rushing wind. It filled the house, then filled the people. That wind was not symbolic. It was power. It was the breath of God reviving ordinary people for an extraordinary calling. The same disciples who had once hidden in fear now stood boldly and preached the gospel with fire. That is what the breath of Heaven does. It takes the timid and makes them fearless: it takes the broken and makes them bold.

You may be weary from the weight of trying to appear strong. You may be holding your breath, just trying to make it through one more day. That is not what you were created for. God has not called you to live strangled by shame or silenced by fear. You were made to live fully alive in His presence. His breath brings clarity. His breath brings courage. His breath brings joy.

David understood this when he cried out in Psalm 119:25, "I am laid low in the dust; preserve my life according to Your word." He knew that only the Word of God could breathe life back into his weary soul. Scripture is not just instruction, it is inspiration, which literally means "God-breathed." When we open our Bibles with open hearts, we inhale what Heaven has exhaled.

There is a reason why the enemy fights to keep you out of the Word and out of prayer. He knows that where the Spirit breathes, chains fall. Where the Spirit breathes, the fire returns. The devil is not afraid of religious activity. He thrives on us using scripture against each other. He is terrified of people who carry the breath of God. He knows that one breath from Heaven can undo years of bondage. One moment in God's presence can realign a weary heart. One whisper from the Spirit can awaken a sleeping soul ready to live a life of God's mercy and grace to those around us.

We need more than good content. We need a fresh wind of God's presence to blow through our hearts, our homes, and our churches. We need to stop pretending that we are fine and start asking God for His help again. The bravest thing you can do is admit your need. Confess your dryness. Cry out for wind. God never withholds His fire from the hungry. He delights in pouring refreshment on those who are desperate enough to ask.

The prophet Ezekiel saw this with his own eyes in a vision of a valley filled with dry bones. God asked him, "Son of man, can these bones live?" Ezekiel replied, "Sovereign Lord, You alone know." Then God told him to prophesy breath. As he obeyed, the Spirit of God entered the bones, and what was once dead stood on its feet, a vast army. That is what revival looks like. It is not emotional noise. It is the power of God breathing on what was dead until it lives again.

You may feel like those bones. Forgotten. Scattered. Lifeless. You may wonder if joy can return or if purpose can rise from your ruins. I think right now, you know, God says yes. Not through willpower, but wind. Not through striving, but Spirit. He does not ask you to fix yourself. He asks you to position yourself for His breath.

Return to stillness. Return to repentance. Return to His Word and create space. Remove distraction and let go of every weight that has suffocated your worship. Clear the lungs of bitterness, compromise, pride, and fear. Let the renewing start.

CHAPTER 4

Revival Starts with Repentance

Repentance is not a shameful word. It is a beautiful one. It is not a punishment or a religious burden. *It is a gift.* It is the moment when the eyes open, the heart softens, and the soul turns. Repentance is not just saying, "I'm sorry." It is saying, "I'm coming back." It is a turning, not merely from sin but toward God.

There is no revival without repentance. No fire without cleansing. No awakening without the breaking of pride. As much as we long for joy, passion, and power, the gateway to every authentic move of God is the same. It is repentance. This word, so often misunderstood and sometimes avoided, is the very ground where the flame of revival is lit.

2 Chronicles 7:14 is one of the most quoted verses about revival, yet it is often treated as a slogan rather than a strategy. It reads, "If My people, who are called by My name, will humble themselves and pray and seek My face and turn from their wicked ways, then I will hear from heaven, and I will forgive their sin and will heal their land." The healing does not come before the turning. The breakthrough does not come without the breaking.

Revival is not something we can manufacture with great music or emotional moments. It is something that heaven pours out in response to surrendered hearts. God is not moved by performance. He is moved by humility. Revival begins when people stop pretending they are fine and start falling on their knees in desperation.

Repentance is not just for the lost. It is for the Church. It is for the pastors and the worship leaders. It is for the mothers and fathers, the students and the workers, the bold and the broken. Repentance is for those who have drifted in ways that no one else sees. It is for those who carry secret compromise while lifting public hands. It is for those who feel far from God but have never stopped serving. He is not angry. He is calling you back. That is what revival is... a return.

We see this clearly in the life of David. When the prophet Nathan confronted him over his hidden sin, David did not resist or deny. He repented. His cry in Psalm 51 is raw and beautiful: "Have mercy on me, O God, according to Your unfailing love; according to Your great compassion blot out my transgressions. Create in me a pure heart, O God, and renew a steadfast spirit within me." David was not trying to clean himself up. He was throwing himself on the mercy of God. That is true repentance. It does not excuse. It does not hide. It surrenders.

There is no revival without this kind of humility. We can sing louder, preach harder, and build bigger, but if we are unwilling to repent, there will be no fire. There may be energy, but there will not be holiness. There may be noise, but there will not be transformation. Revival is not for those who want inspiration. It is for those who want to be cleansed. God will not pour out His Spirit into vessels that refuse to be emptied first.

John the Baptist came preaching repentance before Jesus stepped onto the scene. His message was simple: "Repent, for the kingdom of heaven has come near." Before the miracles, before the signs and wonders, before the cross, there was a call to repent. That order still matters. Repentance makes room. It prepares the way.

In Acts 2, when Peter preached on the day of Pentecost, the people were cut to the heart. They asked, "What shall we do?" Peter replied, "Repent and be baptized, every one of you... and you will receive the gift of the Holy Spirit." The gift followed the turning. The power followed the surrender. There is always more of God to experience, but there is always something we must first release.

The truth is many of us carry things that are choking the flame. Bitterness, hidden sin, unforgiveness, pride, spiritual laziness, secret shame, all of these are weights that smother what the Spirit wants to ignite. God will not force His presence into places we refuse to open. Revival begins when we stop managing our brokenness and start confessing it.

Repentance is not a one-time event. It is a lifestyle. It is the rhythm of a heart that remains soft before God. It says, "Search me. Correct me. Lead me." It is not fear-driven. It is love-driven. When we realize how kind and holy God is, we do not want to stay distant. We want to come close. Repentance is how we draw near. James 4:8 says, "Draw near to God, and He will draw near to you. Wash your hands, you sinners, and purify your hearts, you double-minded." God wants nearness, not performance. He wants truth in the inward places.

Many are praying for revival in their church, their city, and their generation. The cry is beautiful, but revival must begin in private before it is seen in public. It begins with you. In your home. In your thoughts. In your secret places. It is not flashy... it is holy. It is weeping on your floor with conviction. It is letting go of what you justified for too long. It is refusing to settle for closeness to God's work without closeness to God's heart.

Some revivals of history began with crowds. Others began with a single person on their knees. The Welsh Revival began with a young man named Evan Roberts who could not stop crying out for God to break in. His prayers were not polished. They were desperate. He longed for holiness. He longed for the Spirit to move. God heard. God answered. Thousands were swept into repentance. Churches were filled, not with emotionalism, but with reverence. People walked into rooms and immediately began to weep, not because of a program, but because of the presence of God.

That kind of revival is still possible. It is not a thing of the past. It is the heartbeat of God. He is ready to pour out His Spirit again. He is ready to set hearts on fire again. The question is not, "Will God move?" The question is, "Will we repent?"

You do not need to wait for a perfect atmosphere. You do not need a special event. You need a broken spirit and an open heart. Psalm 34:18 says, "The Lord is close to the brokenhearted and saves those who are crushed in spirit." The fire falls where the altar is built. Let your heart be that altar.

Get low. Get honest. Get hungry. Let the tears fall. Let the pride break. Let the old habits die.

This is where revival begins.

This is where you begin again.

CHAPTER 5

The Reformation: Awakening to the Word

In every generation where God has moved in power, one pattern remains constant: His people return to His Word. Revival does not begin with a new sound, a new method, or a new strategy. It begins with the ancient truth spoken by the eternal God. When hearts are awakened to the Word, the fire falls. When the truth is uncovered, the chains break.

Centuries ago, the Church was in a state of spiritual darkness. Truth was hidden behind tradition. Scripture was locked away from ordinary people, guarded in a language only the elite could read. Faith had become a system of fear. Grace was buried beneath performance. God was seen as distant, angry, and unreachable. The people were starving for truth but had no bread. They were parched for life, yet the well was sealed shut.

Then came a young monk named Martin Luther. He was not trying to start a revolution. He was simply trying to find peace with God. In his search, he turned to the Word. As he read the book of Romans, something exploded in his soul. The truth was clear and powerful. Salvation was not something to be earned. It was a gift. Romans 1:17 declared it boldly: "The righteous shall live by faith." Those words burned in his spirit. They broke centuries of religious bondage with one swing of the sword of truth.

Luther's rediscovery of Scripture lit a fire that spread across nations. He nailed his convictions to the church door, not as an act of rebellion, but as a call to return. That single act sparked what we now call the Reformation. It wasn't merely a historical movement. It was a spiritual awakening. The Word of God had returned to the center, and the fire of revival followed.

What made this revival different was not noise or emotion. It was the power of truth reclaimed. Luther decided to ride a new movement: to translate God's Word into the common language. He defied the authorities of his time and worked to ensure that all were empowered to stand for what they believe, to properly believe, not only in God, but in themselves. People began reading Scripture for themselves. They began seeing God, not as a cold judge, but as a loving Father. They discovered grace, mercy, and the beauty of repentance. The flame spread because the truth was no longer hidden. The Bible was printed, preached, translated, and treasured.

That same fire is available today. The Word of God has not lost its power. It is still living and active. It is still sharper than any double-edged sword. It still cuts through deception, division, and despair. In a time where opinion is often louder than truth and emotion is often elevated above doctrine, we need the Word more than ever. We do not need shallow encouragement. We need sacred authority.

Too many believers have settled for secondhand Scripture. They rely on sermons, devotionals, and social media quotes to feed their souls. While those can be helpful, they are not enough. You were never meant to survive on someone else's fire. You were created to hear God's voice for yourself, to open His Word and encounter His heart. The Reformation was not about rebellion. It was about access. Jesus tore the veil, and the Word made the way. You can come close. You can read, learn, listen, and be transformed. And you can empower others to do the same.

Psalm 119 is a love song to the Word of God. Verse 130 says, "The unfolding of Your words gives light; it gives understanding to the simple." There is power in the unfolding. The more we read, the more light enters our hearts. Darkness cannot stay when truth walks in. Confusion loses its grip. Lies are exposed. The soul begins to burn again.

When revival comes, Scripture takes its rightful place. It becomes more than words on a page. It becomes the breath in our lungs, the fire in our bones. In Jeremiah 20:9, the prophet said, "His word is in my heart like a fire, a fire shut up in my bones. I am weary of holding it in; indeed, I cannot." That is what revival looks like, when the Word is so alive in you that you cannot contain it.

We are living in a time when truth is often redefined, twisted, or ignored. Culture will always try to rewrite what God has already spoken. That is why we need the Word more than ever. Not selectively. Not occasionally. We need the full counsel of God, preached with boldness, received with humility, and lived with passion.

The Reformation taught us that every believer has the right and responsibility to engage the Word. It is not reserved for pastors or scholars. It is not confined to seminaries or stages. It is yours. God has spoken, and He wants to speak to you still. Every revival that is sustained over time must be rooted in Scripture. Emotional moments can fade. Charisma can fail. Only truth will remain.

If your heart feels cold, if your passion has faded, if your fire is flickering, start here. Open the Word. Ask God to speak. Let Scripture read you while you read it. Approach it with hunger, not just discipline. Ask the Holy Spirit to ignite your understanding. You will not leave unchanged.

The Word of God is not optional for revival. It is the foundation. It is the flame. Without it, we drift. With it, we burn. It gives us language for worship, direction for life, and conviction for holiness. It comforts the broken, convicts the proud, strengthens the weak, and anchors the wandering.

What began with Martin Luther in a dark and fearful age can continue in our own. Not because of history, but because of hunger. Revival is waiting to erupt again through people who reawaken to the truth of God's Word. You do not need to be famous. You do not need to be flawless. You need to be open. You need to be willing to trade spiritual survival for holy surrender.

Do not settle for vague spirituality.

Do not let culture disciple you.

Do not allow apathy to win. Return to the Word.

Open your Bible.

Hear His voice.

Let it cut.

Let it heal.

Let it burn away the lies and awaken what has gone quiet.

The fire that once sparked reformation can still spark revival in you. That flame has never gone out.

The Word is still alive, and God is still speaking.

CHAPTER 6

The First and Second Great Awakenings: Hearts Set on Fire

Long before megachurches, microphones, or modern worship, there was a movement of God that could not be contained. No stage, no spotlight, and no marketing strategy birthed it. The First and Second Great Awakenings began in places few were watching, through people many had overlooked, and spread like wildfire because the Spirit of God breathed on hearts that were hungry for holiness.

The First Great Awakening swept through the American colonies in the early 1700s. Churches had grown cold. Faith had become formal, stale, and intellectual. People sat through sermons without being stirred. The fire had faded, but a cry began to rise. It was not a cry for emotionalism. It was a cry for truth, for holiness, for the nearness of God. That cry became the matchstick that lit an entire generation.

At the center of this awakening were voices like Jonathan Edwards and George Whitefield. Edwards was not flashy. He was a quiet, deeply theological man who trembled at the weight of God's glory. His most famous sermon, "Sinners in the Hands of an Angry God," was not shouted with charisma. It was read in a monotone voice. Yet the moment he spoke, the room shifted. People began to weep. Some collapsed under the conviction of the Holy Spirit. Others cried out, asking what they must do to be saved. This was not manipulation. It was visitation.

Something holy filled the atmosphere. It was the kind of weight only the Spirit can bring. A deep awareness of God's majesty. A sudden clarity of one's sin.

A hunger for righteousness. These were not emotional waves. They were spiritual awakenings. Entire towns were shaken. Churches were filled. People began living differently, not because of pressure but because of presence.

George Whitefield was another voice of fire. A powerful preacher with a thunderous voice and a burning heart, he would preach to thousands in open fields. There were no microphones, yet people would gather from miles around, standing in rain or snow to hear the Word of God thunder from his lips. Whitefield did not preach self-help. He preached the gospel. He called sin what it was. He exalted the cross. He wept as he preached and watched as thousands wept in response.

The First Great Awakening reminded the world that true revival does not come through human strategy. It comes through holy surrender. It comes when conviction replaces comfort and when the fear of the Lord silences the fear of man.

Decades later, in the early 1800s, the Second Great Awakening began to unfold. This movement was marked by even greater urgency. The flame had dimmed again, but God wasn't finished. He never is. In places like Kentucky and New York, the fire began to fall once more. Camp meetings lasted for days. People gathered under trees, in tents, or wherever they could to pray, worship, and cry out for mercy.

Charles Finney emerged as a bold voice in this second wave. A lawyer turned preacher, he preached with piercing clarity and uncompromising truth. His sermons cut through tradition and exposed the heart. Finney believed that revival was not a random event but a response to repentance. He would say that revival was simply "the renewal of the first love of believers, resulting in the awakening and conversion of sinners." He did not rely on theatrics. He relied on the Holy Spirit.

During these meetings, people often fell to the ground under the weight of conviction. Not because of emotional hype, but because the presence of God was undeniable. People trembled. They shouted. They repented. Lives were changed. Communities were transformed. Taverns shut down. Marriages were restored. The fruit was visible, lasting, and deep.

What made the Great Awakenings

so powerful was not the giftedness of the preachers, though they were indeed bold. It was the brokenness of the people. It was the prayer behind the scenes. It was the hunger that refused to settle. These were not moments of hype. They were moments of heaven meeting earth through the trembling hearts of ordinary people.

The awakenings were not without opposition. Religious leaders mocked the emotion. Intellectuals scoffed at the displays of repentance. Yet the fire continued to spread. That is the nature of true revival. It will never please everyone. It is messy. It is raw. It upsets systems and breaks through walls. Revival always offends the comfortable before it heals the broken.

We need that fire again. Not a replica of the past, but the same Spirit, moving in our time, through our generation. We need churches that cry out like the early Americans did. We need leaders who preach with tears again. We need people who stop asking for comfort and start begging for holiness. God is willing. The question is whether we are ready.

Many believers today long for revival but

resist repentance. We want God to move but do not want to be moved ourselves. We ask for fire but are unwilling to make an altar. The Great Awakenings remind us that the cost of revival is surrender. It is hours spent in hidden prayer. It is hearts laid bare. It is sin confessed, and idols torn down. It is the Word of God exalted above every opinion and trend.

What could happen if we returned to that posture? What would shift in our cities if we stopped entertaining and started interceding? What if our gatherings became upper rooms instead of stages? What if our churches became altars again?

The same Spirit that fell in New England and across the frontier still moves today. He is not tired. He is not distant. He is waiting. Waiting for people who hunger for His presence more than applause. Waiting for churches that will not water down truth. Waiting for young voices to rise and old hearts to burn again.

You do not have to be a preacher to carry revival. You need only be a vessel. The awakenings were carried by people with jobs, families, fears, and flaws. They were not perfect. They were simply willing.

They let the Word break them. They let the Spirit fill them. They let the fire fall.

God is still looking for those kinds of people. Not polished, popular, and perfect... just hungry.

May our hearts be awakened like theirs. May we tremble under truth. May we preach like Whitefield, pray like Finney, and hunger like the nameless crowds who knelt in fields and cried out for mercy.

The flames of yesterday are not enough for today. Let God start a new fire in you.

Let Him set your heart on fire again.

CHAPTER 7

The Jesus Movement: From Counterculture to Christ

Revival has never belonged to the polished. It has never asked permission from the religious elite or waited for the perfect moment. It often comes where no one expects it. That is what happened in the 1970s, when God ignited a wildfire in the least likely place, among the rebels, the wanderers, and the hippies. It was not born in a cathedral or within a committee. It was born in a broken generation, crying out for truth in the middle of cultural chaos. It was called the Jesus Movement.

The world at the time was in turmoil. The Vietnam War raged. Protests filled the streets. Families fractured under the weight of political tension and generational division. The sexual revolution was redefining morality, and drug culture was seducing a whole generation. Churches, for the most part, did not know what to do with it. Many young people had given up on religion altogether, having seen only rules and hypocrisy. Yet beneath the rebellion was a cry. A longing for something real. A thirst for peace that no drug could satisfy. That is where God met them.

The Jesus Movement was not planned. It was not produced by a marketing campaign or launched by a brand. It began when young people started encountering Jesus, not as a religious figure, but as a living Savior. Long-haired, barefoot, countercultural kids began repenting in the streets, worshiping on beaches, and gathering in homes with nothing but a Bible, a guitar, and the fire of God. It was raw. It was messy. It was beautiful.

At the center of this movement

were people who had been radically transformed. They were not just attending church. They were becoming the Church. They came out of darkness and into light, and their gratitude showed. Worship was not performance. It was personal. Many of them knew what it felt like to be bound by sin, gripped by addiction, or numbed by emptiness. When they met Jesus, their surrender was total. Their lives bore the fruit of real repentance. The Holy Spirit filled them with boldness, and they could not stay quiet.

One of the defining features of the Jesus Movement was how quickly it spread. Without social media or livestreams, word traveled fast. People could not explain what was happening, but they knew it was real. Thousands were baptized in the ocean. Churches that opened their doors to these new believers began to overflow. The rigid structures of religious formality were being shattered by the simplicity of the gospel. It was not about programs. It was about presence. It was not about reputation. It was about redemption.

Leaders like Chuck Smith, Lonnie Frisbee, and others became unlikely shepherds of this revival. Chuck Smith, a conservative pastor, opened his heart and his church to the hippies—people others had rejected. What he saw shocked him. These kids were hungry for God. They wept in worship. They devoured the Word. They evangelized with boldness. He did not try to tame them. He taught them, discipled them, and gave space for God to move. Lonnie Frisbee, a charismatic and flawed young man, became one of the early voices God used to call others into repentance and power. His story, though complicated, reminds us that revival often comes through those who are willing, not perfect.

This movement emphasized two things that remain essential for revival today: the power of the Holy Spirit and the authority of the Word of God. These young believers longed for spiritual gifts but also craved biblical truth. They did not separate experience from doctrine. They pursued both. They wanted to feel God's nearness and understand His commands. Their hunger for Scripture was contagious. Their prayers were bold. Their evangelism was radical.

The Jesus Movement gave birth to what many call modern worship music.

Songs written from authentic encounters with God began pouring out. These were not commercial hits or industry products. They were declarations of love, freedom, and surrender. Simplicity marked the sound, but glory marked the spirit behind it. People were being discipled not only by sermons but by song. Every melody was a confession. Every lyric was a testimony.

Revival, in this case, did not wait for approval. It knocked on the back door of the Church and said, "Let me in." Some opened their doors. Some closed them. Yet the fire still spread. It reached across denominations, across states, across cultural lines. It proved again that the Spirit of God does not care about tradition or trend. He responds to hunger.

What made the Jesus Movement different from a momentary trend was the transformation it produced. Former addicts became leaders. Runaways became worshipers. Rebels became preachers. Many of the churches and ministries that exist today trace their roots back to what God did in that window of time. It was not just a flash. It bore fruit.

There are many today who were shaped by those days. Yet God is not finished.

Revival is not a memory to honor. It is a fire to carry. The same Spirit who ignited a generation in the middle of national crisis can do it again. The question is never, "Will God move?" The question is always, "Will we make room?"

We are living in a time that mirrors much of what the 1970s looked like. Culture is confused. Identity is fractured. People are angry, addicted, and spiritually empty. Yet beneath the chaos, there is a cry. There is a hunger for something real. There is a longing for peace, purpose, and truth. This is revival territory. The soil is ready. The desperation is rising. We must not be afraid of the mess. We must not turn away from the broken. Revival always begins where people are desperate enough to say, "Jesus, You are all I want."

Let us not stand on the sidelines while another generation cries out for help. Let us be the ones who open the door. Let us be the ones who say, "Come as you are, but don't leave the same." Let our churches be more like hospitals than museums. Let our gatherings be more like upper rooms than concerts. Let our faith be more like theirs: raw, bold, and burning.

The Jesus Movement proved that revival does not need polish. It needs purity. It needs presence. It needs people willing to let go of control and let God lead.

If He did it before, He can do it again. The fire has not gone out. It waits for the willing.

So, open your heart and make space for the prodigals. Tear down the walls and lift up the name of Jesus.

Let revival come again.

Let it come through you.

CHAPTER 8

Personal Encounters That Change Everything

When heaven draws near, and the living God is standing right in front of you, without a doubt, you know it is sacred and unmistakable. Those moments do not leave you the same. One encounter with the presence of God can do what years of routine religion never could.

The Bible is full of these divine disruptions. They are not grand entrances reserved for the elite. They are quiet, holy invasions into the lives of flawed, ordinary people. God did not wait for Moses to be perfect before He appeared in the burning bush. He came to him while he was hiding in the wilderness, unsure of who he was and convinced his past disqualified him. The bush burned with fire but was not consumed. That was not just a sign, it was a message. God was saying, "I will put fire in you that does not destroy you. I will give you My presence, and it will carry you where your ability cannot." From that moment on, Moses was changed. He went from a fugitive to a deliverer. One encounter rewrote his entire future.

Isaiah had a similar experience. He was already a prophet. He already knew the temple. Yet in Isaiah 6, he has a vision that shatters him. He sees the Lord, high and lifted up, and the train of His robe fills the temple. Angels cry out, "Holy, holy, holy is the Lord Almighty." Smoke fills the room. The weight of glory is unbearable. Isaiah immediately cries, "Woe to me! I am ruined! For I am a man of unclean lips." This is what happens when God comes close. We do not boast in our goodness, we tremble in His holiness. Yet God does not crush Isaiah. He cleanses him. A burning coal touches his lips, and a commission follows. "Whom shall I send? Who will go for us?" Isaiah answers with trembling obedience: "Here am I. Send me."

Personal encounters are always twofold. First, they purify. Then, they propel. God never shows up just to give us a feeling. He shows up to realign us, to remove what does not belong, and to call us into purpose.

The woman at the well in John 4 met Jesus in the middle of her shame. She was not seeking Him. She was avoiding the crowd, showing up at noon when no one else would be there. Yet Jesus was waiting for her. He did not condemn her. He offered her living water. He saw her past, acknowledged her present, and revealed Himself to her with stunning clarity. "I am He," He said when she spoke of the coming Messiah. That one moment with Jesus turned a rejected woman into a bold evangelist. She ran back to her village, proclaiming, "Come, see a man who told me everything I ever did."

This is what happens when God comes close. We are known and transformed. His glory is revealed in the very place where we were once silenced by shame.

The wounds we tried to hide become testimonies of His grace. A single moment with God can ignite a lifetime of purpose.

Encounters with God are not confined to biblical times. They are for today. Right now.

We often think we need to do more to get close to God. Yet the truth is, He is already near. James 4:8 says, "Draw near to God, and He will draw near to you." The act of drawing near is not about proximity. It is about posture. It is about putting down the distractions, humbling ourselves, and becoming honest again. Encounters begin with surrender. God will not force His way into a hardened heart, but He rushes into a humbled one.

The early Church was born from an encounter. In the upper room, 120 people waited, prayed, and obeyed. Then, like the roar of a mighty wind, the Holy Spirit came. Tongues of fire rested on them. The timid became bold. The fearful became fearless. That moment marked them forever. They were no longer just followers of a memory. They were carriers of presence.

Revival cannot be sustained by borrowed fire. It must be personal. It must be deep. It must be real. You cannot live off someone else's story. You must have your own. One moment of true encounter will do more for your faith than years of religious effort. It will drive you to your knees in awe and lift you to your feet in power.

Some avoid encounters with God because they fear what He might expose. Others avoid them because they do not believe He will show up. Still others think they are not worthy. The enemy whispers, "You've gone too far. You've been too inconsistent. You are too broken." None of that is true. God has never required perfection to reveal Himself. He has only ever looked for hunger.

The blind man in John 9 encountered Jesus and walked away seeing. The thief on the cross encountered Jesus and walked into paradise. The prodigal son returned home and encountered the embrace of a father who ran to meet him. These were not perfect people. They were desperate people. They were willing. They were open.

God is still the same. Still drawing close. Still interrupting schedules to capture hearts. Still turning runaways into revivalists.

CHAPTER 9

Burn Again

In Revelation 2, Jesus commends the church in Ephesus for their hard work, perseverance, and refusal to tolerate evil. From the outside, they looked faithful and strong. Yet Jesus, who sees beneath the surface, says something that cuts deep. "Yet I hold this against you: You have forsaken the love you had at first." Other translations call it "your first love." That passionate, joyful, childlike, pure love. The kind that doesn't calculate or perform.

The kind that doesn't worry about what others think. The kind that just wants to be close.

Jesus doesn't shame the Ephesian church. He invites them to remember, repent, and do the things they did at first. Revival is not about chasing a feeling. It is about rekindling a relationship. It is about coming back to the One who loved you when you had nothing to offer.

First love is fierce. It says yes before asking questions. It weeps at His feet, not to be seen, but because nothing else matters. First love gives generously, worships freely, and obeys quickly. It has no reputation to protect. It just wants Him. That kind of love is not meant to be a memory. It is meant to be the foundation.

When we drift from our first love, we do not always run into rebellion. Often, we settle into religion. We keep serving, doing, producing, even keep going to church. Yet our hearts grow distant. We substitute effort for intimacy. We say the right words, but something inside feels numb. Our hands are busy, but our hearts are bored. Doing and going become a checklist. Often we also settle into the world. Into the culture. We dumb down our words because they might offend, and, sometimes, we truly believe it's because we don't *want* to offend.

That is not how we were meant to live.

God never designed us for a cold faith. Nor is He impressed by performance. He is moved by passion. In Deuteronomy 6:5, the greatest commandment is clear: "Love the Lord your God with all your heart and with all your soul and with all your strength." Not just believe in Him.

Love Him with everything.

The beauty of returning to your first love is that you don't have to start from scratch. You just have to turn around. Like the father running to the prodigal son, God meets you the moment you take a step. His love is not waiting to be earned. It is waiting to be embraced.

If you have lost your fire, do not ignore it. It is sacred. It is the whisper of the Spirit calling you back. That longing is proof that the fire is not dead. It is simply waiting for breath. You don't need a conference to stir it. You need a moment of surrender.

Go back to the beginning. Go back to the place where you first met Him.

Where were you? What were the circumstances?

Remember the wonder. Remember the tears. Remember the way His presence undid you. Remember how you didn't care who was watching or what they were thinking. You just wanted Him.

In the current world where posts on social media and public interaction is a mainstay, we overlook the one mainstay that matters. When we refocus on that, everything else lines up.

Jesus.

Sometimes we need to return to the things we did when our faith was fresh. We need to wake up early again, not out of duty, but desire. We need to sing when no one is around. We need to open the Bible not to check a box, but to hear His voice. We need to pray like He's in the room, because He is.

The fire returns when we return. Not in a flash of emotion, but in steady rekindling. Flame by flame. Moment by moment. Word by word. He restores what we thought we lost. He renews what we thought had faded.

In Psalm 51:12, David cries out, "Restore to me the joy of Your salvation." This is not a shallow request. It is a desperate plea. David knew what it meant to feel distant. He had experienced the consequences of compromise. Yet he also knew the mercy of God. He knew that revival was possible. He knew that deep joy could return.

Your joy can return too. The passion you had at first is not gone forever. The love that once moved you to tears is not lost. God knows how to restore the fire. He knows how to breathe life into dry places. He knows how to awaken love again.

The Church doesn't need more spectacle. It needs more first love. It needs more hearts undone by the beauty of Jesus. More people who love Him for who He is, not just what He does. When first love is restored, everything changes. Worship comes alive. The Word pierces deeper. Prayer becomes intimate. Sin loses its grip. Fear loses its voice in your head.

Do not settle for going through the motions. Do not let your faith become a routine. God has more for you.

Cry out for first love again. Make space. Strip away every distraction. Ask Him to take you back to the place where it all began. Lay down the pride, the disappointment, the fear.

Remember what it was like to worship with nothing to lose.

CHAPTER 10

A Life That Invites Revival

Keep in mind, revival is not meant to be an occasional event. It is not a weekend service, a guest preacher, or a song that gives you goosebumps. Revival is a lifestyle. It is the ongoing, burning reality of God's Spirit breathing through your daily life. A life that invites revival is one that chooses surrender over spectacle and obedience over emotion. It chooses approval from God over the approval of others.

It is easy to crave moments. We want the upper room without the waiting. We want fire without the fuel. We long for fresh encounters but often resist the daily habits that keep the flame burning. The truth is, revival cannot be microwaved. It is cultivated. It grows in the soil of faithfulness, watered by worship and nourished by the Word.

Romans 12:1 urges us to present our bodies as living sacrifices, holy and pleasing to God. That is what true worship looks like. Not just singing on Sundays, but laying down our entire lives on the altar. Revival is not just what happens when the Spirit falls. It is what happens when we keep showing up with hearts that say, "Here I am, God and I worship You with everything."

This is where the real fire lives. Jesus withdrew often to lonely places to pray. He met the Father not just in public moments but in private devotion. He showed us that the strength to carry power in public comes from intimacy in private. Without the secret place, we are spiritually fragile, constantly needing the next high to feel alive. With the secret place, we are rooted, ready, and steady, no matter what comes.

It thrives not in perfection, but a posture that says, "God, remove anything in me that grieves You." Holiness is not legalism. It is love. It is a response to His goodness. It is a desire to stay close. Psalm 24:3–4 asks, "Who may ascend the mountain of the Lord? Who may stand in His holy place? The one who has clean hands and a pure heart." Purity positions us for deeper encounters. It protects the fire.

Living a life that invites revival also means guarding what we consume. We cannot expect to carry heaven if we constantly feed on what dulls the Spirit. What we watch, what we listen to, what we scroll through, it all shapes us.

Prayer is the oxygen of revival. Not polished prayers, but persistent ones. Revival has always been birthed through intercession. Those who pray regularly carry a fire that cannot be manufactured. You do not have to be loud or eloquent. You just need to be honest. Cry out. Plead for your generation. Weep for your family. Contend for your city. God still answers the prayers of the desperate.

Community is also vital. Revival is not meant to be carried alone. The early

Church in Acts was a revival community. They broke bread, prayed together, shared everything, and saw God move daily. We need people who fan our flames, not extinguish them and vice versa. Surround yourself with people who stir your hunger, who speak life, who challenge you to go deeper. Revival becomes contagious in community.

Obedience is the firewood of sustained revival. The Spirit will fall where He is welcomed, but He remains where He is obeyed. A lifestyle of revival is one where we say yes to God, no matter what it costs. He may ask you to forgive someone you want to avoid. He may ask you to give when it stretches your faith. He may call you to leave something behind so you can carry more of Him. Revival cannot coexist with partial surrender. The fire falls on sacrifice.

Do not underestimate the power of small, unseen choices. The decision to wake up early and open your Bible. The moment you choose to worship instead of worry. The quiet act of kindness when no one is watching. These are seeds of revival. God sees every one of them. Nothing done in faith is wasted.

We must stop chasing a revival "moment" and start becoming revival people. Those who burn whether the lights are on or not. Those who carry the presence of God into the grocery store, the classroom, the office, and the dinner table. A life that invites revival is not loud for attention. It is loud with love. It leaks the fragrance of Jesus into every environment.

Revival people are known for their humility. They do not seek credit or recognition. They know that the fire is not from them. It is through them. They deflect the glory and magnify the One who made the ashes burn again. They are not trying to be impressive. They are trying to be available.

2 Timothy 1:6 reminds us to "fan into flame the gift of God." That flame needs tending. Let your life become an altar. Let your words be incense. Let your choices become oil for the flame.

CHAPTER 11

Carriers of Fire

The Holy Spirit did not fall in the upper room so the disciples could stay hidden. He fell so they could go *boldly*. The fire came to move them from prayer to proclamation, from waiting to walking, from silence to boldness. What began in an upper room in Acts 2 could not be held there. Peter stepped out and preached with power. Thousands were saved. The gospel began to spread like wildfire, not because the disciples were brilliant strategists, but because they were burning with the presence of God.

Revival has a ripple effect. It starts with one but never ends with one. If the fire stays in the church building, we've missed the point. We are not called to be keepers of the flame. We are called to be carriers of it. We carry it into conversations. We carry it into culture. We carry it into conflict. We carry it into dark places where light is needed most.

You do not need a microphone to be a carrier of revival. Many often think, "well, I do not have a platform." But we all do. Our platform is our life itself. God has us where we are for a reason, It doesn't have to be on a stage. You only need a surrendered heart. You do not need a title. You need availability. God has always used the unexpected to bring about the extraordinary. He used fishermen, tax collectors, shepherds, and teenage girls. He is not looking for "impressive." He is looking for *willing.*

Being a carrier of fire means we refuse to compartmentalize our faith. We do not turn it on and off based on location or audience. We live it. We let it leak through everything. How we speak, love, forgive, and serve. The fire of revival is not just emotional passion. It is holy obedience. It is a life that shines so brightly that people see Jesus before they ever hear His name.

Jesus said in Matthew 5:14–16, "You are the light of the world. A city on a hill cannot be hidden... Let your light shine before others, that they may see your good deeds and glorify your Father in heaven."

Carrying fire looks like joy in the face of sorrow. It looks like peace in a storm. It looks like integrity when no one is watching. It looks like compassion when others are cold. It looks like truth spoken in love and grace extended even when it's hard. You do not have to be loud to burn. You just have to be *real*. People recognize real. They recognize fire.

The early Church, as described in the book of Acts, didn't revolutionize cities through marketing tactics but through fearless faith. Their actions included healing the sick, feeding the poor, expelling demons, and preaching about Jesus with conviction and clarity. Their goal wasn't to win over the world. They were trying to obey the One who set them free.

Acts 4:13 says, "When they saw the courage of Peter and John and realized that they were unschooled, ordinary men, they were astonished and took note that these men had been with Jesus." That is what marked them. Not their education or resume. Presence. That is what marks every carrier of revival. They have been with Him. They have encountered the fire, and it shows. It burns to light the way.

People are searching for truth, identity, hope, and healing more than ever. The world is desperate for it. Culture is loud with confusion, and the Church must respond, not with noise, but with power. Not with empty words, but with lives that burn with the character and compassion of Christ.

A revival life is not always convenient. It will cost you. It may stretch you. It will certainly require you to choose courage over comfort. You may be misunderstood. You may be mocked. You may even feel alone. You may even die for it. Yet you won't care.

You will call it all glory.

CHAPTER 12

Until the Whole Earth Is Filled

Habakkuk 2:14 declares a vision that pulses with divine urgency: "For the earth will be filled with the knowledge of the glory of the Lord as the waters cover the sea." That is the endgame. That is the promise. Not pockets of inspiration or random sparks. A world soaked in the knowledge of who God is, covered with His presence, overflowing with His glory.

We must see revival through the lens of eternity. What God begins in a moment of repentance, He wants to spread across nations. What He awakens in you is meant to awaken others. The Holy Spirit was never given just to make us feel alive. He was given to make us witnesses. Acts 1:8 makes that clear. "You will receive power when the Holy Spirit comes on you; and you will be My witnesses... to the ends of the earth." Revival that does not reach outward is incomplete. It must go. It must move. It must spread.

God has always moved through fire with global intention. The fire that fell at Pentecost in Jerusalem didn't stay there. It spread to Samaria, Antioch, Ephesus, Rome, and beyond. The gospel moved through borders, languages, and barriers because the people carrying it believed that the message was too good to keep. They were not only revival recipients, instead they became revival messengers. The gospel didn't advance because of structure. It advanced because of fire.

If you burn but do not share the flame, the fire eventually dies. God calls us to be vessels and voices. The revival God is pouring out now is not just for emotional renewal. We are not called to simply survive until Jesus returns. We are called to burn until the whole earth knows.

There are people who have never heard the name of Jesus. Entire tribes, cities, and nations are still waiting for light to break into their darkness. There are people dying a spiritual death in the world of confusion. A world filled with constant changing standards and decline. God is not content with partial fulfillment. He wants the whole earth filled with His glory. He is stirring hearts in every corner of the world right now. In underground churches in China, on dirt floors in Uganda, in tiny apartments in the Middle East, in college dorm rooms across America, revival is stirring.

You are not separate from that. You are a part of it. The same fire that burned in Moses' bush, the same fire that fell in the upper room, the same fire that swept through revivals in Wales, Azusa Street, and Argentina, lives in you. The Spirit of God does not localize. He multiplies. What starts in your life has the power to affect your neighborhood, your city, your nation.

Global revival begins with individual obedience. The Great Commission is not optional. It is the calling on every believer's life. It may look different for each of us. Some are called to go. Others are called to give. Some are called to preach. Others are called to intercede. Yet all of us are called to burn. None of us are excused from the urgency of eternity.

Jesus said in Matthew 24:14, "This gospel of the kingdom will be preached in the whole world as a testimony to all nations, and then the end will come." That means revival is not just a blessing. It is a signal. When the gospel spreads and nations awaken, the return of Jesus draws near. Revival hastens the day.

We live in a time of global shaking. Wars rage. Economies collapse. Morality decays. Fear spreads. Good becomes bad and bad becomes good. People are dying daily for standing on the word of God. It's here. And it is not the time to retreat. It is the time to rise. The darker the world becomes, the brighter our flame must shine. Jesus called us the light of the world. That light must be visible. It must be undeniable.

Carrying revival into the nations begins with carrying revival into your home. Your children, your spouse, your neighbors, they are all your mission. The mission field is not only across oceans. It is across your table. Start there. Then ask God to expand your reach. Ask Him to send you where the fire is needed most. Whether that means across the street or across the world, say yes.

There is no such thing as small obedience. Every step you take in the Spirit moves the Kingdom forward. Every time you say yes to God's prompting, the fire spreads. You may never preach to a stadium, but your flame will still change the world. One prayer can unlock heaven over a household. One conversation can shift a soul toward eternity. One spark can ignite a revival in a place you'll never see but God never misses.

This is undeniably not the time to grow passive. It is absolutely not the time to be lukewarm. This is the definitive hour to burn alive. The earth is crying out. People are desperate for Truth. Heaven is ready to move.

And you were born for such a time as this.

ABOUT THE AUTHOR

Michelle Jester is a former Crisis Counselor and Public Relations Consultant, in conjunction with working in publishing for twenty-plus years. She spends her time writing in addition to maintaining her full-time publishing career. An author of fiction, nonfiction, and children's books, Michelle is also a contributing author to the #1 bestseller, My Labor Pains Were Worse than Yours.

She lives in Louisiana with her husband, high school sweetheart and retired Master Sergeant. Michelle wears a bracelet every day with a single, yellow, rubber duckie charm on it to remind her to enjoy the fun and happy things of life!

Feel free to connect with her, and sign up for her monthly newsletter: MichelleJester.net